WHEN PRAISE MEETS WORSHIP

The Workbook

NAKIA O. SHY

Published by:
Ellis & Ellis Consulting Group, LLC
954-439-0760

Cover Design:
Paul Ellis
Ellis & Ellis Consulting Group, LLC
954-439-0760

Editors:
Sara E. Little and Cheron Maddox

Photography:
Obasi Studios | www.obasistudios.smugmug

ISBN 13-9781793388551

Printed in the United States of America.

Behold, how good and pleasant it is
when brothers dwell in unity!
It is like the precious oil on the head,
running down on the beard,
on the beard of Aaron,
running down on the collar of his robes!
It is like the dew of Hermon,
which falls on the mountains of Zion!
For there the LORD has commanded the blessing,
life forevermore.

Psalm 133

TABLE OF CONTENTS

May the God of endurance and encouragement grant you to live in such harmony with one another, in accord with Christ Jesus, that together you may with one voice glorify the God and Father of our Lord Jesus Christ. Therefore welcome one another as Christ has welcomed you, for the glory of God.

Romans 15:5-7

Introduction

Wow! I cannot believe you are holding this workbook in your hands. Just as it was said about Jesus, *'Can anything **good** come out of **Nazareth**?' Philip said to him, 'Come and see.'* (John 1:46). I want you to take a journey with me into the life of a country girl from New Bern, North Carolina. I want you to see what can happen when you push past fear.

This workbook is the culmination of a vision God gave me back in 2016. As a self-proclaimed educator, I love to see the light bulb moment happen, and workbooks make me happy. It is through this workbook that application happens. Far too often, we read a book that is full of great nuggets, but we do not know how to apply what we have just read.

I did not want to write another book that did not give the reader a means to put into action what they read. Additionally, I have been asked on numerous occasions how I study and what tools I use. This book will take you on a journey to help you not only go deeper in the worship arts ministry, but it will also teach you how to study the word of God for yourself.

It has been an interesting journey over the past year. I would have never thought that in the span of one year I would publish a book and begin writing this companion workbook. When writing ***When Praise Meets Worship (WPMW),*** my idea was to make it interactive, and to make it unlike any other book written on dance. After many months of toiling over the pages, the book was birthed.

This workbook will allow you the space to explore further what you have already learned. If you have not read ***When Praise Meets Worship,*** I highly encourage you to do so. Although my desire was to have a stand-alone workbook, there is so much foundational information that would be beneficial. If you have read it, utilize this workbook to take you deeper. I do not just mean deeper in the word of God but deeper in your introspection. This workbook will challenge you to take a look in the mirror. That look will produce a better understanding of who you are as a worship arts minister. That look will produce a security in your identity.

So, sit back, grab a pencil and your Bible, and get ready to challenge yourself. Do not worry; you are truly up for the challenge. The fact that you purchased this book is testament to that readiness.

Chapter 1
I Know Who I Am

Have you ever asked yourself who you are and wondered why you are here? Perhaps you felt drawn to the ministry of dance but did not know why. I would even go so far as to say that some of you are dancing but are not sure if you are truly called to the ministry. This confusion could be due in part to the fact that you do not know who you are. Yes, you know your name, you know your gender, and you even know what job you have, but your identity goes far beyond that.

When dealing with identity we must start at the beginning. Before you were born, someone determined that you needed a name. Your parents, uncles, aunts, family friends, or even neighbors weighed their options and came up with what they deemed ideal. As you read the Bible you find many cases, if not all, where names had a direct correlation to one's character.

Who are you? List five words that describe who you are.

____

____

____

____

Now list five characteristics that don't include your marital status, parental status or job title.

____

____

____

Read Genesis 29
According to Genesis 29:34, what does the name Levi mean?

____

____

Read Exodus 32
What characteristics did the tribe of Levi demonstrate that in this chapter that aligns with the meaning given in Genesis 29? Be sure to be as detailed as possible.

____

____

____

____

____

____

____

What is the origin of your name?

____

____

What is the meaning of your name?

____

____

What character traits does your name relate to?

____

____

____

____

____

____

How does the meaning of your name correlate to your life experiences?

____

____

____

____

____

____

Reflect over the last 10 years of your life and list situations that lends itself to meaning behind your name.

____

____

____

____

____

____

Some of you might not like what you found. Some of the names chosen for you were not ideal. Some are adjectives that are contrary to who God called you to be. I say change the name you answer to, just as Abram's name was changed to Abraham. That name change aligned with the purpose God had for him. Jacob's name was changed to Israel, Saul to Paul. Change the name that you answer to. We as worship ministers are called to function as a type of Levite. Just as the Levites of old assisted the congregation in their worship, so is your charge. We assist them with their sacrifice of worship; we demonstrate God's word, and what it is currently saying. It is by our function that we are attached to God. Answer to that name and align with what that name describes you to be.

Now that you know what your name means we will now identify who you are as a minister of movement and worship leader. Below you will be asked to provide definitions for a few words. Please be as thorough as possible with your definitions. You may want to utilize a traditional dictionary, concordance, and Bible dictionary. Each resource may give you different insight into each word.

MINISTER

____

____

____

____

MOVEMENT

____

____

____

____

WORSHIP

____

____

____

____

LEADER

DANCE

I am sure you are wondering how those definitions came close to defining how you as a worship leader. Metaphorically speaking, as a minister of movement you are a member of the tribe of Levi. From an assignment structure, the Levites were charged with assisting the children of Israel with their sacrifices, which was, in part, how they worshiped.

According to *When Praise Meets Worship,* when was movement/dance first used and in what capacity?

According to Exodus 32 why was the tribe of Levi chosen to serve God closely?

____

____

____

____

____

____

What are the three parts of the Tabernacle of Moses?

____

____

____

I find it interesting that God established man in three parts; there are three parts to the God-head and therefore three parts to worship. God does not do anything haphazardly. Everything created or instituted has a purpose. This triune approach to worship provides balance, much like a three-legged barstool. This is to say each leg/aspect of worship is not only important individually but needed to fully support the weight of the glory of God and the assignment of the worship service itself. If one part is missing it has a noticeable impact on the worship service, as well as the worshipper.

Ecclesiastes 4:12 *And though a man might prevail against one who is alone, two will withstand him—a threefold cord is not quickly broken.* (ESV)

Take the remainder of this chapter to write down some areas of your identity you want to explore further. Determine which areas of your identity require a deeper level of study and where you would like to see yourself within the next 5-10 years.

____

____

____

____

____

____

____

____

____

____

____

____

ADDITIONAL NOTES

Chapter 2
Do You See What I See?

Prophetic ministry may be new to some but extremely familiar to others. Over the past several years there has been an increased emphasis on prophets and the prophetic. I promise you I was equally confused and intrigued when I began my prophetic journey. As mentioned in ***WPMW,*** every minister of movement should be prophetic. As you continue your study, it will become evident how important it is to understand and flow in this area.

In order to make sure we are all on the same page, let us define a few things. A common mistake in a believer's understanding and vocabulary is to confuse prophesy with prophecy. Although they are similar they are not the same.

DEFINE PROPHECY

____

____

____

DEFINE PROPHESY

____

____

____

God does not speak to all prophetic people in the same manner. Some people are highly visual; they get prophetic revelation through visions and sometimes dreams. They tend to describe their prophetic encounters using the words "I see." Others are audible; they are able to hear their prophetic revelation OR begin to speak and are not aware of what is being said.

Define the following terms:

NABY

____

____

____

RA'AH

____

____

____

CHOZEH

____

____

____

Based upon the above words where do you fit in? Write down the last time God spoke to you. How did it come about?

____

____

____

____

____

____

Perhaps you do not fit into the above. I know of one prophet with whom God uses all five senses to convey information. When she smells certain scents she knows they represent God's presence. She is also able to taste things, often times metallic. I say all of that to emphasize we serve a God who is not one dimensional. Do not worry if you do not hear, see, feel, taste or smell. God can manifest himself in whatever fashion he shall choose. That does not make you greater or lesser, just uniquely made.

Read 2 Chronicles 15:27

What type of prophet was Zadok?

____

____

____

Based upon what you read what is unique about this type of prophet that would be beneficial as a worship leader?

Most of us like to hear a word from God, but rarely are we taught how to respond to that word. As prophetic movers, we are to not only demonstrate what God is saying but also how to respond to that word. Take a moment to go outside and watch nature. If able, go to a place where you see trees.

Now that you are there, describe what happens to the tree when the wind blows. Describe what you see the leaves do. The branches. If the tree has needles or fruit, what happens to those? Is it alive or dead? If alive, is it a sapling or a mature tree?

What season (winter, spring, summer, fall) are you observing this tree in? I would recommend you go back to the same spot during each season and annotate the subtle changes in response that happens. Please write those observations here.

____

____

____

____

____

____

Did you notice that each time the wind blew, the tree had a physical response to it? Did you notice that response differed depending upon the season? Let us take it a step further and look at a garden or flower bed. When it rains, something happens to the soil. The water penetrates the soil and finds its way down to the roots which provide nourishment to the plant. Once the nourishment is received the plant begins to respond. The stage of growth will determine how rapid and to what extent the response will be. Let us also not forget how the sun impacts this cycle.

Now you might ask, "Why is she going so deep with nature?" We are much like a plant or tree when it comes to the supernatural. There should be a response to any prophetic word or atmosphere we encounter. As ministers of movement, when God says there is a river flowing, not only are we to demonstrate the river, but we should also demonstrate how to respond to the river.

What impact does a river have on the landscape around it?

____

____

____

____

What comes to mind when you think of a river spiritually?

____

____

____

Briefly describe what happens when a river crests or exceeds flood stage limits.

____

____

____

____

____

____

How should we respond to a spiritual river?

____

____

____

____

____

____

Not only is it vital that we position ourselves to be able to receive prophetically from God but to also provide the appropriate answer or response. Keep in mind that there is more than one way to receive or respond prophetically. What is important is that we position ourselves to in a manner that allows us to receive and respond.

Ideally, at this point, you have identified how you receive: audibly, visually, or through one of the other senses. I cannot reiterate enough that one method is not superior to another; all are needed. We all have the same Holy Spirit flowing in us, but we may have different administrations. Each one brings his or her piece to the overall puzzle that makes the picture come to life. Take a moment to reflect on what you have discovered in this chapter. Be sure to detail how God speaks, when he speaks, and how you physically respond to his presence.

ADDITIONAL NOTES

Chapter 3
The Preparation

This chapter is the most important of the entire book. Many want to launch out into the deep but fail to ensure that they can handle the deep. Getting to the deep is the easy part; the hard part is sustaining the depth. Can you swim? Do you know how to tread water? Are you even able to float? All are necessary skills as it relates to navigating the deep. I know, I know; you are probably going to talk about how Peter got out of the boat and was fine until he began to doubt. I am so happy you brought that up. You see, Peter and the eleven others missed a perfect opportunity. Jesus was the Rosetta stone which they should have studied, but study without application is useless. They walked with Jesus, had an idea of who Jesus was, but it was not until that moment that they were tested to see how much they had retained. How much did they truly understand the person of Jesus? Plus, Jesus knew he would not always be present in the flesh. He needed them to be able to walk without him. Jesus was the master teacher.

DIET/PHYSICAL FITNESS LOG

I want you to log your physical activity as well as your food intake over the next ten days. Please do not alter your normal activity. Include how much water you drink. Oh, I know that tea, soda, sports drinks, and Crystal Light have water in them; however, for this exercise only log how much pure water (no flavor added) that you consume. Also, log (record) the amount of sleep you get each night. Typically, we do not think of sleep as part of physical fitness. However, studies have shown that individuals, especially women, have a more difficult time losing weight when they consistently get less than six hours of sleep per night. Include the time you get into the bed, how much time you spend doing activities that interfere with your sleep/rest cycle (reading, watching television, social media, etc.).

Day 1:

Breakfast

____

____

Lunch

____

____

Dinner

____

____

Snack

____

Water Intake (Total Ounces) ________________________

Physical Activity/type/duration/intensity

____

____

Sleep/rest cycle

____

____

Day 2:

Breakfast

____

____

Lunch

____

____

Dinner

____

____

Snack

____

Water Intake (Total Ounces) ________________________

Physical Activity/type/duration/intensity

____

____

Sleep/rest cycle

____

____

Day 3:

Breakfast

____

____

Lunch

____

____

Dinner

____

____

Snack

____

Water Intake (Total Ounces) ____________________________________

Physical Activity/type/duration/intensity

____

____

Sleep/rest cycle

____

____

Day 4:

Breakfast

____

____

Lunch

____

____

Dinner

____

____

Snack

____

Water Intake (Total Ounces) ____________________________________

Physical Activity/type/duration/intensity

____

____

Sleep/rest cycle

____

____

Day 5:

Breakfast

____

____

Lunch

____

____

Dinner

____

____

Snack

____

Water Intake (Total Ounces) ________________________

Physical Activity/type/duration/intensity

____

____

Sleep/rest cycle

____

____

Day 6:

Breakfast

____

____

Lunch

____

____

Dinner

____

____

Snack

____

Water Intake (Total Ounces) ____________________________________

Physical Activity/type/duration/intensity

____

____

Sleep/rest cycle

____

____

Day 7:

Breakfast

____

____

Lunch

____

____

Dinner

____

____

Snack

____

Water Intake (Total Ounces) ________________________

Physical Activity/type/duration/intensity

____

____

Sleep/rest cycle

____

____

Day 8:

Breakfast

____

____

Lunch

____

____

Dinner

____

____

Snack

____

Water Intake (Total Ounces) __________________________________

Physical Activity/type/duration/intensity

____

____

Sleep/rest cycle

____

____

Day 9:

Breakfast

____

____

Lunch

____

____

Dinner

____

____

Snack

____

Water Intake (Total Ounces)____________________________

Physical Activity/type/duration/intensity

____

____

Sleep/rest cycle

____

____

Day 10:

Breakfast

____

____

Lunch

____

____

Dinner

____

____

Snack

____

Water Intake (Total Ounces)____________________________

Physical Activity/type/duration/intensity

____

____

Sleep/rest cycle

____

____

REFLECTION

After taking the time to log your eating and fitness routines, what insight did you gain?

What patterns did you notice with your behavior and time?

On average how much water did you drink?

____

____

____

On average what was your rest cycle? Was it adequate? Do you wake up feeling rested or drained?

____

____

____

Take a moment and make an honest assessment of your current activity level. Think about how often you minister through dance. Answer the below questions honestly.

Does your current fitness level adequately prepare your body to minister effectively? If not, why?

____

____

____

Do you experience fatigue after five minutes or more of moderate activity?

____

____

____

Are you currently able to dance to an up-tempo music set for more than seven minutes without needing to take a break or feeling like you need a medic?

____

____

____

____

Do you currently and consistently exercise or participate in strenuous activity for more than thirty minutes that causes your heart rate to increase outside of rehearsal or ministry assignments? If so list those activities? If not, what is your plan to get there?

____

____

____

____

Is the time you spend exercising greater than the time you spend ministering or preparing for ministry?

____

____

____

If you have answered no to three or more of the above questions, your activity level does not support your call to minister effectively before God's people. Not maintaining your physical condition limits how well and how often God can use you. Your assignment is to assist the congregation with their sacrifice of worship. How effective can you be if you are not able to stand as long as required?

Fortunately, there are practical ways to increase your activity even if you suffer from physical limitations. First things first, begin to move. Increase your activity level gradually. Please do not read this workbook and then try to run a marathon if you have not properly trained for it. Simply commit to doing better. Increase your steps by parking your car farther from the door at your job, the mall, and grocery store. Take an exercise class twice a week. Bottom line, get moving. **NOTE: Please consult your physician before starting any increased or new physical activity.**

LEAPING FROM SCRIPTURE

Leaping from scripture is merely putting your study in motion. This exercise can be handled in many different ways. This section will give you a few ideas on how to implement this valuable exercise to increase not only the vocabulary of your ministers of movement but also their confidence. Many dancers feel a level of anxiety when asked to participate in spontaneous worship because in their minds they do not know what to do. They find themselves locked in a state of inadequacies that are often self-imposed. This exercise is also valuable when teaching your ministry how to flow prophetically or during worship service.

First things first: we must begin with some definitions. What I want you to do is look up the following words in the dictionary but also in the concordance. We want the English, Hebrew, and Greek definitions of these words. For the English definition, write whether it is a noun, verb, adverb, etc. For the Hebrew and Greek, list the name, *Strong's Concordance* number as well as the definition. Be mindful that you might have more than one number associated with the word. **NOTE: Please utilize the King James Version when looking up scripture in the concordance.**

DEFINITIONS

GLORY

List five scriptures referencing the word Glory.

____

____

____

____

____

____

Dictionary ____

____

____

Hebrew ____

____

____

Greek ____

____

____

MAJESTY

List five scriptures referencing the word Majesty.

____

____

____

____

____

____

Dictionary ________________________________

____

____

Hebrew __________________________________

____

____

Greek ___________________________________

____

____

HOLY

List ten scriptures referencing the word Holy.

____

____

____

____

____

____

Dictionary ______________________________________

____

____

Hebrew ____

____

____

Greek ____

____

____

RIGHTEOUS

List five scriptures referencing the word Righteous.

____

____

____

____

____

____

Dictionary ______________________________________

____

____

Hebrew ____

____

____

Greek ____

____

____

WONDER

List five scriptures referencing the word Wonder.

____

____

____

____

____

____

Dictionary ______________________________________

____

____

Hebrew ____

____

____

Greek ____

____

____

HONOR

List five scriptures referencing the word Honor.

____

____

____

____

____

____

Dictionary ______________________________

____

____

Hebrew ______________________________

____

____

Greek ______________________________

____

____

WORTHY

List five scriptures referencing the word Worthy.

____

____

____

____

____

____

Dictionary ______________________________________

____

____

Hebrew ____

____

____

Greek ____

____

____

WORSHIP

List 15 scriptures referencing the word Worship.

____

____

____

____

____

____

Dictionary ________________________________

____

____

Hebrew ___________________________________

____

____

Greek ____________________________________

____

____

ACTIVATION

Let us start with moving to these words before we go into actual scripture. Break the ministry up into groups and give them a word. Define the word based upon the dictionary, the Hebrew, as well as Greek. Give each group five minutes to come up with movement that depicts that word. An alternative is to give the entire ministry the word. Allow each member to show you a different movement for said word. This will cause each member to think purposefully about the word in question. This individual demonstration is not recommended for a large ministry, especially if the members are not actively enrolled in dance class. Encourage them to utilize their space and allow for a combination of movements to fully express each word.

Be mindful that individuals will state that the person or persons that presented movement prior to them used the movement they wanted to demonstrate. Continue to encourage them to demonstrate a variation of the same movement.

You now have a great baseline for scriptures to not only study but to use for this exercise. We cannot properly display what God is saying during worship when we do not have a full understanding of what we are demonstrating.

A word of caution: do not attempt to get through the entire list at one rehearsal. Ensure care and encouragement are given during this activation. This activity will be the first time that many of your members have danced with everyone looking. Some will withdraw and shut down. This is to be expected, so encourage them through the process. You may have to dance with them the first time to get them started.

After you have completed this activation, ask the ministry members what they thought about the exercise. Remain open to the feedback as some members may not have enjoyed this activation. This does not mean you should not continue as this is part of the growth process.

REFLECTIONS

Now that you have gone through this exercise, lets journal your thoughts.

How did this exercise make you feel?

____

____

____

____

____

____

____

____

____

If you are the ministry leader, what did you observe from your ministry members?

If you are a ministry member, what did you find encouraging about this exercise?

How did this exercise make you grow?

Open communication is vital for growth and development. Leaders, give your members an opportunity to express their feelings or concerns regarding this exercise. Be prepared for both positive and constructive feedback. You may find this exercise was not received well initially, but your members grew to like it. Some will not like this no matter how often you do it. Just because it is not liked does not mean it is not necessary for growth. Growth is often uncomfortable; I am sure diamonds are uncomfortable during their formation process.

This next section will not require definition but will deal with concepts that are common during worship service and that will definitely come up during prophetic worship. The best thing to do when you do not know the song is to dance the word. Unfortunately, many of us do not have a balanced study life. What I mean is that most of us tend to focus on one particular area or theme and do not often delve into another unless circumstances call for it.

In this next section, list five or more scriptures related to the keywords given. Be sure to list scriptures from both the Old and New Testaments.

VICTORY/TRIUMPH

____

____

____

HEALING

____

____

____

WAR/WARFARE

____

____

____

THE PROMISES OF GOD

____

____

____

ACTIVATION

Choose either one of the scriptures listed above or a Psalm. I suggest you start with the book of Psalms. The authors of the Psalms take the reader through almost every emotion and adjective used to describe God, an issue that we face today. This is a sure foundation to build upon.

Once chosen, have a member of the ministry read the passage. Read it slowly enough for the movement minister to articulate the scripture. Encourage them not to attempt to dance each word but more so the sentence or theme. The idea is to paint a visual picture of the meaning of what is being said and not each word being said. If the movement minister is uncomfortable or cannot find his or her way, begin to define what those words mean. Sometimes it is hard to demonstrate what we do not fully understand. Be mindful that some individuals will say they cannot do this "right". This exercise is not about right or wrong but freedom of expression and opening them up to a new method of doing so.

If you are the movement minister, relax. Do not take the activation so literally or seriously. I remember the first time I did this. I found myself thinking entirely too much. I was so trapped in my thoughts that none of the movement I thought I was doing actually happened. Over time it got easier. I became comfortable not only leaping from scripture but dancing during spontaneous worship. Exercises like this prepared me to be a worship leader. Although graced by God to do this, it is the preparation that allows me to make it look easy.

REFLECTIONS

Now that you have gone through this exercise as a worship ministry take a moment to journal your thoughts.

How did this exercise make you feel?

____

____

____

____

____

____

____

____

If you are the ministry leader, what did you observe from your ministry members?

____

____

____

____

____

____

If you are a ministry member what did you find encouraging about this exercise?

How did this exercise make you grow?

REHEARSAL TIME

This is the part of ministry that is extremely important but often neglected. Trust me, we will make sure to have rehearsal, but the neglect comes in how we go about it. We tend to only come together to learn our notes or choreography. Often times we merely come together out of obligation. The true development of the minister or ministry is often secondary to the day-to-day grind of producing for the house. Ministry development requires strategy. The majority of the issues that the ministry has can be resolved during this time of deliberate fellowship. Rehearsal is the perfect time for building relationships and should be a safe place for vulnerability.

This next section will help give proper context to your current rehearsal construct and hopefully give you a baseline on some areas that can be improved. In order to shed some light, please take a moment to answer the following:

How long is a rehearsal and how often do you meet?

____

____

____

____

____

Describe a typical rehearsal.

____

____

____

____

____

____

____

____

Answer the following based upon your description of rehearsal:

Did it start on time?

____

Was it organized? If no please explain.

____

____

____

____

____

____

Was any time given to word study?

____

____

Was time given for warm up? If so, how much time and what is typically done?

____

____

____

Was time allotted for free or spontaneous worship?

____

____

How much time is typically spent doing nonproductive things and what are they?

____

____

I totally get that you have limited time when it comes to rehearsal. If you take a look back over your last three rehearsals, you may find that you are spending a great deal of time doing things unrelated to rehearsal. Perhaps rehearsal does not start on time. Perhaps you spend twenty minutes talking about things unrelated to ministry. Maybe the rehearsal was not organized, so you spent time trying to decide what song to minister or arguing over choreography. Being unorganized will cause you to waste valuable time that could be used to develop the ministry. The following are some suggestions to better maximize the limited time you have together:

1. WARM-UP/STRETCHING

Set aside about ten to fifteen minutes to properly warm the body up. I like to do an up-tempo song to get the body ready for stretching. Strategically work muscle groups from head to toe in that order. Warm the neck up with neck rolls, followed by shoulder rolls, then add in arm circles. Be sure to do the reverse of whatever movement you do. Next, you want to warm up the waist/torso by moving it clockwise and counterclockwise. Be mindful to stretch the lower back.

Lower body stretches can and should take longer as you have larger muscle groups to consider. Do not just focus on your calves, quadriceps, and hamstrings. Make sure you work on the hip/hip flexor as well as the glutes. Many athletes, dancers included, have been injured due to tight glutes. We end with warming up the ankles.

During warm-up, make sure your stretches are what we call dynamic, which means they require movement like jumping jacks, running in place, or ballet barre work.

List five songs (title and artist) for warm-up.

____

____

____

____

Write down a series of movement for warm-up that address the areas mentioned above.

____

____

____

____

____

____

____

____

2. STRENGTH TRAINING/CONDITIONING

This is my favorite part of rehearsal as it prepares the body to endure the weight of our assignment. Some of the activities I would suggest are jumping jacks, burpees, planks, pushups, lunges, squats, running in place or around the sanctuary, arm circles, bridges, dips, calf raises, tendu' series, plie series, and crunches.

Write down a series of movement for training/conditioning that address the areas mentioned above. Be sure to include the number of repetitions for each movement.

____

____

____

____

____

____

3. BIBLE STUDY

Part of getting to know those who labor with you is studying together. Bible study should be as deliberate and structured as the choreography. Allocate a specific and predictable amount of time to Bible study during each rehearsal. Assign either a designated chaplain to conduct study or rotate this requirement. This will stretch your ministry not only in the Word, but it will also give them a safe place to demonstrate their ability to facilitate Word study. Make sure that you set a schedule and outline what the Word study will consist of. Schedules are key to success; no one should be told at the last minute they need to prepare to teach.

Ecclesiastes 3:1 – For everything there is a season, and a time for every matter under heaven.

We serve a God that is concerned about order and timing which means we serve a God that is structured and strategic in all things. Apply that same level of structure and strategy to your ministry, Word study, and development.

Write out a draft study schedule for the next three-six months.

____

____

____

____

____

Now that you have a schedule, let us delve into selecting study topics. Each ministry or individual are in different places spiritually. Additionally, you want to be in line with not only the needs of the ministry but the flow of the house/church you are part of. The below questions will assist with picking study topics.

What topic area has the pastor or senior leader been teaching?

____

____

What is the annual theme/vision of the church?

What are some of things/issues that the ministry is battling? List them and write down some key scriptures pertaining to those areas.

Have you done a study on spiritual gifts? If not list some questions and/or scriptures concerning spiritual gifts.

Are there special topics requested by ministry members? If so what?

____

____

____

____

____

____

The above questions should have given you much to think about and a great foundation to begin or continue grounding your ministry in the word.

Use the below section to solidify your study topics for the next six months.

____

____

____

____

____

____

____

____

4. CHOREOGRAPHY

Before going into choreography, there should be teaching, which can be done during Bible study, as to the significance of the song, biblical foundation, and vision for the piece and how it fits into the worship service. Many of us minister to songs that we like or that perhaps speak to us directly but have very little to do with the direction of the house. Keep in mind that all ministry should collectively set an atmosphere that is ripe for the word of God to come forth. Each ministry and ministry member has a mandate to assist the man or woman of God in the delivery of God's message. We should set an atmosphere that is pliable. We should till the ground so the seeds of the word can fall on the fertile soil of the hearts of the congregation and take root. It should be so in line with where the Holy Spirit would like to go that it should shift the service as Holy Spirit directs. So, we should take great care to not only select the correct song but also ensure that our choreography speaks clearly what heaven is saying.

Below you will find a song selection worksheet that I developed for a previous dance ministry. At least twice a year, each minister of movement had to present a solo piece. The purpose of this piece was to assess the minister of movement and provide feedback. This worksheet allowed me to determine if their desired message and what was conveyed were the same. It also was the ideal time for them to provide me with feedback on how they have assessed themselves and how I could help them grow.

SONG SELECTION WORKSHEET

Name of song, artist, and length.

____

____

List scripture(s) the song is based upon.

____

____

What type of song (Worship, Travail, Praise, Deliverance, Prophetic etc.)?

____

____

What is the message of the song (Try not to utilize the wording/phrases of the song)?

____

____

____

At what type of event or setting would this song minister best?

____

____

How danceable is the song for you or your group?

____

____

____

What type of dance best fits the song (worship, travail, warfare)?

____

____

____

What movement type best fits this song (lyrical, modern, ballet)?

____

____

____

What color garment best conveys the message of the song and why?

____

____

____

What do you see when you hear the song?

____

____

____

____

____

____

What instruments could be utilized to bring clarity to movement or message?

____

____

____

____

____

5. FREE WORSHIP

This is perhaps my favorite part of rehearsal time as it allows each minister of movement an opportunity to freely be who they are. This gives space for them to tap into their own worship experience while providing an opportunity to learn how their fellow ministry members worship. This exercise, if done frequently, will provide insight into how each member naturally flows through worship. It will also provide invaluable information for the ministry leader and members as to what type of dancer each member is, as well as which ministers naturally flow together and which ones need to learn how to flow with one another.

NOTE: I suggest you initially utilize music that is known to the ministry/dancer. This will ease them into worshiping freely in front of others. As they become more comfortable, introduce the individual or individuals to less familiar music. This will prove to be invaluable if you are ever ministering with a prophetic worship team.

ACTIVATION

Select a slow worship song. Have one dancer begin to minister alone. Allow them to minister alone, even if uncomfortable, for about 30 seconds to a minute then add a second dancer. Allow them to minister together for about a minute then signal the first dancer to leave. Allow the second dancer to minister alone and repeat the process until you get through the ministry. Pay close attention to the entire interaction to determine if the ministers of movement were responsive to their surroundings.

What did you notice?

____

____

____

____

____

____

____

____

____

____

What types of movement did you see?

Was it hard or difficult to match the movement types?

Describe the type of interaction that happened when you began to minister together.

Describe the eye contact with your partner? If lacking how did you, or could you, overcome it?

____

____

____

____

____

____

____

Were you distracted by their movement? If so what made it distracting?

____

____

____

____

____

____

Note: a song is considered worship based upon the words not upon the tempo. It is possible to have a slow praise song or a fast worship song.

REFLECTIONS

How did this exercise make you feel?

____

____

____

____

____

____

____

____

____

If you are the ministry leader, what did you observe from your ministry members?

____

____

____

____

____

____

____

____

If you are a ministry member, what did you find encouraging about this exercise?

____

____

____

____

____

____

____

How did this exercise make you grow?

____

____

____

____

____

6. LEAPING FROM SCRIPTURE

This was discussed in detail earlier in the workbook. This is the ideal time to take the ministry, including the leader, through this exercise.

How are you responding to this exercise?

After doing this a few times describe how your attitude towards it has changed?

Do you find it easier to go through it now? Explain

How has your personal and collective ministry changed because of this exercise?

Describe the confidence level of the ministry or you individually.

7. COOL DOWN

This is probably one of the most vital parts of rehearsal that is commonly neglected. The cool down takes the muscles that have just been used, stretched, strained, and worked for over an hour and gives them room to release some of the built-up toxins. ***Note these toxins are called lactic acid. Lactic acid is the source of soreness you experience when you either begin utilizing muscles that have been dormant or when you increase the intensity of muscle use. The more you use the muscles, the less the acid builds up resulting in decreased soreness**.

Now that your muscles are warm from movement, you can do some static stretches. These stretches are generally held between 20 and 30 seconds.

I would recommend playing some slower tempo music such as instrumental pieces to allow the body to fully relax. Begin with the neck and work your way down the body. Start with neck rolls, then down to the shoulders and upper back. Make sure you stretch the lower back, then move down the body until you get to the ankles. You will then need to stretch your glutes and groin. Yes, the muscles in your derrière are vital to posture, alignment, and sciatic nerve health. Having tight glutes can lead to nerve pain, a weakened core, and inhibited range of motion. Groin stretches help strengthen your ability to leap, kick, turn, and balance. Take special care to stretch your hamstrings as well.

As you can see, there are several major large muscle groups in your lower body. In my travels, I have noticed many dancers with back issues, most of which can be traced to either not executing movement properly, which is why dance class is so important, or not properly warming up and cooling down the body.

List 5 songs (title and artist) for cool down

____

____

____

____

____

____

Write down a series of movement for cool down that address the areas mentioned above

____

____

____

____

____

____

EXAMINE PERSONAL MOTIVES

If you are not the ministry leader, this section is not an attempt to give ammunition to pick apart your leader. On the contrary, this section is a tool that is to be used by you to assist the ministry leader in further developing the ministry. I know many of you may be frustrated with how things are being handled, but I assure you the majority of your leaders genuinely desire to please God and to lead an effective ministry. Many of us do better when we know better. Many of the things listed here are things I had to learn through many failed attempts at getting it right.

If you are the leader, please be encouraged as you go through this section. Many of us who lead unfortunately have not been given the tools to be effective. I also ask that you be open to change. Take the time to see what you have been doing, and see how that can be improved, what needs to be left in the last season, and what new things can you incorporate. God is always doing a new thing, and we must be in position to execute.

Before we can be effective in anything we endeavor to do, we must assess why we are doing it. It is the motive that will encourage us when we are pressed on every side. Our motives are the fuel for everything that we do. Unfortunately, all fuel is not created equal.

Let us relate this to driving a car. Some cars run on unleaded gas while others run on diesel. We can break this down even further. Vehicles that require unleaded gas have three common options: 87, 89, or 93 octane. I once owned a Volvo XC-60. I loved that crossover vehicle. It was roomy, the ride was so smooth, but one thing I was discontent with was she – yes, her name was Simone -- required 93 octane gas. Now, the owner's manual said I could use either 89 or 93. Of course, being the frugal person I was, I tried 89 initially. The vehicle functioned, but it did not run as smoothly. I noticed a delay in responsiveness when I wanted to pick up speed. Something about the ride was just off. One day, I drove her until she was almost empty and filled her up with 93. Immediately, I saw a difference in her performance. She handled like she was supposed to. She could run on 89, but 89 was not ideal. Many of us are performing tasks and engaged in ministry with the wrong fuel but are expecting a pristine outcome. If the motive, or fuel, is not correct the ministry will not function at optimal capacity. Just as selecting the wrong fuel will impact the longevity of a vehicle, the same will happen in ministry if our motives are not correct. Did you know you can cause serious damage to your vehicle if you use the wrong fuel? Imagine what can happen if individuals are on the ministry with the wrong motives: the damage it can cause to ministry as well as to the congregation can be severe.

REFLECTIONS

Why do you want to be part of this ministry?

Are you called to the ministry of dance? If so, in what capacity?

How do you know you are called to this ministry?

____

____

____

____

____

____

____

____

____

What sacrifices are you willing to make in order to be part of this ministry?

____

____

____

____

____

____

____

____

Are you willing to submit for a period of time (time can range from one month to one year) where you are not ministering before the congregation? During this time, you would be expected to participate during rehearsals and any other ministry assignments given by the leader. Describe your feelings concerning this requirement.

____

____

____

____

____

____

____

____

The ministry of dance requires a financial commitment that is not found in many other ministries. Have you considered the financial obligations associated with the ministry?

____

____

____

____

____

____

____

Describe your current prayer life.

____

____

____

____

____

This ministry will require you to rehearse regularly during the week or weekends. It may also require a level of travel and attendance to additional church services both locally and out of town. Does your current home, work, school situation allow for this? Explain.

____

____

____

____

____

____

What do you expect to gain from being part of this ministry? (Spiritually, emotionally, etc.)

____

____

____

____

____

What gifts or skills do you presently possess that will benefit the ministry?

Have you ever been part of a dance ministry before? If so what position(s) did you hold and describe your experiences with that ministry?

What is your temperament?

____

____

____

____

____

____

____

Ministry leaders, do you have an organized and well thought out observation period? This should be structured in a fashion that can be duplicated and not based on personal feeling or relationships. If you have not created one, now is the perfect time to think about those things. Although not all-inclusive, the below questions will help you develop a program.

1. Does your church currently have a new members' protocol for ministries? If so what is it?

____

____

____

____

2. How often do you rehearse and are rehearsals structured to allow you to observe the technical abilities of your members?

____

____

____

____

____

____

3. How active is the ministry? Are you called upon each Sunday? Do you only minister for special occasions? Are you part of praise and worship?

____

____

____

____

____

____

4. Is Bible study and fasting a consistent part of ministry preparation?

____

____

____

5. How important is attendance of church service, Sunday school and Bible study to the ministry?

____

____

____

____

____

____

____

____

____

____

____

____

6. Is there an age limit to join the ministry? Are you structured to have varying age groups in the ministry?

____

____

____

____

____

7. How important is timeliness to the ministry?

8. What are your expectations for any new or current member of the ministry?

9. What can new and current members expect from you as a leader? Include your temperament, work ethic, prayer life, fasting life, willingness to learn new things, etc.

10. What personality types do you have difficulty leading? This question is strictly for you as the leader to consider and overcome not to screen out these personality types. Also, list how you can adjust to better deal with them.

Hopefully, this section was beneficial for the entire ministry. Regardless of where you find yourself in ministry, it is always valuable to assess your motives as well as where you are spiritually. Perhaps your motives were pure when you started, but you now find yourself going through the motions out of perceived obligations. Finally, has God called you to the ministry or is He telling you it is time to move? Remember the Bible is clear, *"Has the Lord as great delight in burnt offerings and sacrifices, as in obeying the voice of the Lord? Behold, to obey is better than sacrifice, and to listen than the fat of rams" (1 Samuel 15:22, ESV).*

PERSONAL STUDY

The amount of time dedicated to personal study will vary from person to person. The one thing that is constant is the need to study. ***"Do your best to present yourself to God as one approved, a worker who has no need to be ashamed, rightly handling the word of truth" (2 Timothy 2:15 ESV).*** This version of this scripture was chosen primarily because the word "study" was replaced with a charge for us to do our part to make sure we are presenting ourselves as approved with the implication that we cannot if we are not able to rightly handle the word of truth. It is impossible to correctly handle the things of God without study.

Study of the word of God is much different from reading the word of God. Reading is just that, reading. Most of us do this in order to learn what the Bible says. Studying the word goes beyond knowledge of the order in which the words appear but rather why they appear. Study of the Bible goes into the culture, demographics, and political and social issues of that time. All of this provides the proper context of the scripture, therefore giving a fuller understanding of what you are reading.

KEY STUDY MATERIAL

PARALLEL BIBLE- Just like the scripture quoted above, different versions of the Bible will give you hidden context to the intent of the scripture being read. I will not begin to endorse one version over the other; however, if you go to any reputable bookstore, they will have a chart that describes each version of the Bible, what its primary use is, and how close it is to the original text. Getting close to the original text is very important as it will have a better rendering of the intent of the wording. The parallel Bible allows you to have more than one translation in front of you for ease of study.

CONCORDANCE- Do not get overwhelmed by the size of the book. The concordance will give the Hebrew and Greek meaning for the words listed in the Bible. The original text of the Old Testament was written in Hebrew while the New Testament was written in Greek. If you are reading a passage of scripture and want to know what a word means, open the first part of the concordance and find the word. Once found, look at the list of scriptures to find the one that contains the word you are seeking. Once located, move over to the right and there will be a number. Flip to the back of the concordance and find the associated number. Looking at the correct section is vital.

BIBLE DICTIONARY- Probably the second most valuable tool after the concordance, the Bible dictionary will not only define a word but give historical information surrounding a word or topic. This dictionary helps you place the context of that particular book of the Bible. It will help you understand the tone and the reasons why that book was written.

CHRONOLOGICAL BIBLE- If you are like me, the Old Testament can be rather confusing. This is partly because the books of the Old Testament are not in order. For example, the book of Job took place during the time of Genesis. Now, why is that important? Well, it gives you a better timeline of what happened and when. Another example is part of the book of Nehemiah happened at the same time as a part of the book of Ezra. When you understand the timeline, the meaning or purpose of the books is much clearer.

APPLICATION

Develop a list of resources you would like to purchase.

____

____

____

____

____

____

____

____

What study material do you currently have?

____

____

____

____

What is your favorite scripture?

____

____

____

____

____

Using your favorite scripture, answer the following questions.

Look up this scripture in at least three different translations and note the differences no matter how subtle.

Pick two key words and look them up in a concordance. List the Strong's number, Greek or Hebrew word, and definition of each.

Looking at the introduction to a book in a study Bible, what is the main theme of this book of the Bible?

What was happening during the time this book was written that impacted the author and why they spoke in that particular tone?

What are some Jewish, Greek, or Roman customs that might have impacted the author?

REFLECTIONS

Now that you have completed this study exercise take a moment and journal what new things you learned.

How would adding this to your personal time with God be beneficial?

____

____

____

____

____

____

____

How can you incorporate this into your ministry?

____

____

____

____

____

____

ADDITIONAL NOTES

Chapter 4
Where You Lead, I Shall Follow

We have come to the point of the workbook that requires not only deep reflection or introspection but also the most flexibility. Hopefully, by now, we have established a solid foundation that we can build upon. Effective leading is a byproduct of our preparation.

Let us first delve into the different types of dance. As mentioned in ***WPMW***, there are about nine different types of dance mentioned in the Bible. Specifically, we have celebration, praise, worship, warfare, intercession, travail, healing, deliverance, and prophetic. We will take a moment to define these different types of dance.

Based upon your reading of ***WPMW***, complete the following:

For this section provide a definition, list two scriptures, and describe what the movement might look like for each type of dance listed below.

PROPHETIC

____

____

____

TRAVAIL

____

____

____

CELEBRATION

____

____

____

WORSHIP

____

____

____

INTERCESSION

____

____

____

PRAISE

____

____

____

HEALING

____

____

____

WARFARE

____

____

____

DELIVERANCE

____

____

____

What types of movement would best fit each type of dance?

____

____

____

What facial expressions best support each type of dance listed?

____

____

____

____

____

____

Define the word "proficient":

____

____

____

Define the word "skilled." Include the Hebrew definition and scripture reference.

____

____

____

____

____

Based upon the definitions provided in *WPMW* and your personal research, which type of dance do you consider yourself to be proficient in and why?

____

____

____

____

____

____

What genre or genres of dance would help you become proficient, or skilled, in the areas you are not currently?

____

____

____

____

____

____

Sometimes while trying to determine what kind of dancer you are, you will have to take a look at what you find yourself naturally doing. I have a friend who is a warfare dancer. It does not matter what song is playing or even if the atmosphere is heavy with worship. She will begin worshiping but always finds herself pacing back and forth, speaking in a heavy set of tongues. She will pick up a mattah or war sticks and begin smiting. The next sets of questions are designed to help narrow down what type of dancer you are naturally. This does not mean you are proficient in these areas, but it will give you a good place to start.

Describe your style of dance. Is it flowy, sharp, etc.?

____

____

____

____

____

____

What type/style of dance do find yourself naturally gravitating toward?

____

____

____

____

____

____

What instruments of worship do you find yourself in love with?

____

____

____

____

____

____

Do you typically use instruments to augment your dance? If so, list them.

____

____

____

____

____

____

Of the nine types of worship dance you previously defined, which one(s) is/are your weak area(s)?

____

____

____

____

What do you find difficult about those areas?

____

____

____

____

____

In order to begin to grow in these areas, you first must begin with a word study of each dance type. You began such a study in the previous exercise; however, we shall go deeper with the following exercise.

For your areas of weakness, add the Hebrew/Greek to your definition. Find the first time that word was used in scripture. What was happening contextually in that scripture? Be sure to find supporting scriptures in both the Old Testament and New Testament. You may not find the actual word in both testaments. For example, you may see the word worship in the Old Testament, but in the New Testament you may see prostrate or vice versa. You will need to open your mind and think creatively. Allow Holy Spirit the opportunity to guide you.

PROPHETIC

TRAVAIL

CELEBRATION

WORSHIP

INTERCESSION

PRAISE

HEALING

____

____

____

____

____

WARFARE

____

____

____

____

____

DELIVERANCE

____

____

____

____

____

This exercise was to give you a better understanding of the nine types of dance mentioned in this workbook. It is hard to be the visual representation of something if we do not truly understand what it is. Now that you have completed your word study, you are better equipped to demonstrate these various types of movement. You may find that some movements overlap. Some of you may have finally found the answer to the question of what kind of dancer you are. Identity is everything. Once you know who you are, you are better able to show forth God's glory in the earth.

Note there are more than nine types of dance. The remainder of this section is provided for you to continue your study.

ADDITIONAL NOTES

POSITIONING AND FORMATIONS

Picking a formation is not difficult; the difficult part is perfecting how you will lead based upon the formation. Many dancers have a hard time leading while looking others in the eye. This is compounded when the formation calls for dancers to face them in the aisle.

Let us take some time to try the two formations mentioned in ***WPMW***. Take special note as to what worked, what did not work, and annotate them in the section below.

Formation one: Place dancers in two or three rows behind the leader. Make sure to stagger the dancers in such a way that the dancers in the second row will not be directly behind the dancers in the first row. When done correctly, the dancers on the first and third rows will be directly behind each other and likewise with the dancers on the second and fourth rows.

Formation example:

			X			
X		X		X		X
	X		X		X	
X		X		X		X
	X		X		X	

**Typically, a fourth row is not used unless the size of the sanctuary calls for it.*

While standing in this formation, have the leader select five to seven different movements or combinations. The formation should follow without verbal instructions or music. Once complete, please answer the following questions:

Describe your placement in the formation.

____

____

____

____

____

____

____

Were you able to easily see and execute the movements? Explain.

____

____

____

____

____

Repeat this exercise with the same leader but change where your personnel are positioned.

Describe your placement in the formation.

___

___

___

Were you able to easily see and execute the movements? Explain

___

___

___

___

___

___

___

Was it easier or more difficult to follow compared to where you were located previously? Explain

___

___

___

___

___

Formation two: Place the majority of your dancers in formation one. Place the remaining dancers in the aisle facing formation one. Be sure to arrange the dancers from shortest to tallest. Your shortest dancer should be the first one facing formation one.

Describe your placement in the formation.

____

____

____

Were you able to easily see and execute the movements? Explain

____

____

____

____

____

____

Was it easier or more difficult to follow compared to where you were located previously? Explain

____

____

____

____

____

Was it difficult having the dancers face you? Explain

____

____

____

____

____

Which placement was ideal for you? Explain why.

____

____

____

____

____

____

Which placement did find to be the most difficult? Explain why.

____

____

____

____

____

I have found over the years that regardless of who is leading, it is easier for me to follow if I am on the right side of the formation. I am visually impaired and have to wear glasses. Like most things, one side of your body is stronger, longer, faster, or more flexible. My left eye is my good eye (it is ok to laugh; I am as I type this). Everyone knows if you want me to be able to follow, I need to be on your right side. It is good to know which side of the formation is your strong side versus your weak side.

TRANSITIONING

If this is an established ministry, it might be beneficial to identify who in the ministry is comfortable with leading worship and/or appears to have the ability to do so. I know you are asking, "Well, how am I supposed to do that?" This is where the "Free Worship" and "Leaping from Scripture" exercises come into play. Mind you, those exercises are not always 100% accurate. What I mean by that is although someone is able to flow well with others they may have a hard time remembering that they are leading a company of dancers. Think back over your previous exercises and answer the following questions.

Did you observe a dancer or dancers who were naturally able to flow or follow other dancers with ease? If so, describe what you saw.

____

____

____

____

____

____

How many of your ministers tend to dance inward? Inward means they tend to close their eyes and forget anyone else is in the room.

____

____

____

____

____

____

____

____

DANCE THE MESSAGE, NOT THE WORDS

This is especially important for an up-tempo song. I will not say praise because we confuse what praise is versus worship. It is possible to have a slow praise song and a fast worship song. By now you have completed exercises in chapter three that should have assisted you in this area. The best way to prepare to dance the message is to begin to leap from scripture. As an educator, one principle has proven to be true: repetition reinforces learning.

ACTIVATION

Select a scripture not previously used for another exercise. The book of Psalms is always a great place to start. Once chosen, have a member of the ministry read the passage. Read it slowly enough for the movement minister to be able to articulate the scripture. It should be easier to dance the phrase or sentence versus individual words. The idea is to paint a visual picture of the meaning of what is being said and not each word being said. Keep in mind that you may need to provide a definition or two in order to assist in putting the scripture into context. Sometimes it is hard to demonstrate what we do not fully understand. Be mindful that some individuals will say they cannot do this "right". This exercise is not about right or wrong but about freedom of expression and opening them up to a new method of doing so.

REFLECTIONS

How did this exercise make you feel?

____

____

____

____

____

____

If you are the ministry leader, what did you observe from your ministry members?

____

____

____

____

____

____

____

____

____

____

____

If you are a ministry member, what did you find encouraging about this exercise?

How did this exercise make you grow?

Chapter four would not be complete without a visual representation of what not to do. Below are several pictures that, although exaggerated, represent things that I have encountered over the past twelve years.

Where can one begin? Dance is a language and should be executed fully. Extend those arms, and notify your face that you are worshiping the Father. Secondly, it is easy to get distracted, but stay focused on the leader. Sometimes we accept the call when we are not fully committed to the ministry. It will show in your efforts or the lack thereof. Lastly, you are part of a group; this is not the time for individual worship.

Although not perfect, this still is a wonderful representation of what it should look like when the dancers are on one accord. The focus here is not on whether the arms are exactly the same height or if the lean is at the same degree but that the heart is poured out to our Father.

Be careful of doing movement directly in front of your body. It is difficult for those behind you to see what you are doing. They are left to try to figure out what is being done and if you are not careful, they will display their confusion in the most hysterical ways.

Ideally, what is done on one side should be done on the other; therefore, the ministers of movement should not have to look back over their shoulder to see what is happening next. Remember, it is perfectly okay to miss the movement the first time it is done. ***WPMW*** outlines signals and patterns which assist not only the leader but the follower on what is coming next.

I have often been asked, "How should we respond when the 'King' enters into the room?". Pageantry is typically used to convey a message, and here we see the crown of the King approaching. The first thing we want to do is acknowledge the entrance. This is only one way to acknowledge Him coming, so whatever you do make sure it is done in reverence.

We want to bow or get low once the King comes near as a sign of reverence and respect. Again, this is merely a demonstration. In the natural, once the King entered we would all stand and then subsequently bow or avert our eyes as he passed by. You see here two of our ladies just did not know what to do, so they just stood there. When in doubt, just bow.

The crown should never be handled like it is a toy or an irrelevant object. Remember, it represents the God of Abraham, Isaac, and Jacob. Arms should be fully extended. I mean even baby girl knows something is very wrong here.

You will never know shoulder pain until you have held a crown aloft for a long period of time. Regardless of how tired you get, know that someone has your back. Each member should be aware of the weight of this glory. Make sure during rehearsal each member gets a chance to hold the crown properly for a period of time. Once they understand the weight, they will never leave someone to hold it for too long. If the person holding the crown is showing signs of fatigue, walk up behind them and offer support for their arms.

What can I say about this foolishness? Why are we fighting to hold the crown? There is a right way to exchange the presence of God, and this is definitely not it. Aside from the awkwardness of it all, my back should not be to the congregation. We cannot expect people to follow us if we are out of order. Those ladies were just as confused as the congregation is going to be if this were to happen.

The proper way to exchange the crown is to come behind the person who is holding the crown. Whisper in their ear if need be to let them know you securely have the crown. Do not move until the crown is stable because we do not want to drop the King. Once the crown is secure, the person in front begins to step forward.

Once the crown has been securely transferred, the person being relieved should still show reverence by bowing as they walk away. I know your arms are sore, shoulders tired, and back tight; however, we are still before the congregation and representing how we are to conduct ourselves in the King's court. Continue to bow until you are either off the stage or platform or back in the formation.

ACTIVATION

By this time, you have completed a detailed study on various forms of worship. You have increased your dance vocabulary by taking dance classes (I know I sound like a broken record). You have selected several movements for common words such as glory, worship, and honor. You have practiced not closing your eyes or looking at the floor. There is only one thing to do now, and that is to put all of your studies into practice.

I want to encourage you that this might seem difficult initially, and that is because you are in your head. You can do this, you will be fine, making mistakes is part of the process. Transparent moment, I make mistakes often. I have lost rhythm, forgot what movement I did for the same phrase previously, signaled that I was turning left and turned right, and the list goes on. I am not talking about several years ago; I am talking about several weeks ago. It happens. I tell dancers all the time it is ok to make a mistake. Consider that your solo moment. If you are going to do a solo, make sure it is prolific and then get back in formation!

EXERCISE

- Break your ministry into groups of three or four. Establish one dancer in each group as the leader.
- Allow the dancers to select the formation that works best for them. ***The leader should step slightly forward as it is easier to see them looking forward instead of the being in a straight line. ***
- Select a song that the ministry is comfortable with. I typically do not use a familiar song as it forces the minister to stretch and will not reinforce comfortable behavior; However, do what is best for your ministry.
- Either have the dancers transition at the end of the song or ask them to transition during the song.
- Continue this format until each dancer has an opportunity to lead and follow.

***Ministry leaders, please read the questions in your reflections section. This will assist you as you monitor this exercise. ***

REFLECTIONS

Now that you have gone through this exercise as a worship ministry, journal your thoughts. These reflections are broken into two sections: one for the ministry member and the other for the ministry leader. I encourage you if doing this as a ministry, to share some of your thoughts as a ministry. Sharing is a growth opportunity that often goes overlooked. We cannot grow together if we do not share with one another.

MINISTRY MEMBERS

How did this exercise make you feel?

____

____

____

____

____

What did you find encouraging about this exercise?

____

____

____

____

Did you find this exercise difficult? If so, how did you overcome those feelings?

____

____

____

____

____

____

Did your movement change as the rhythm, tempo, and message of the song changed? Please elaborate.

____

____

____

____

____

____

____

____

____

Describe your transitions, signaling and patterns. Were they smooth, difficult, confusing etc.?

____

____

____

____

____

____

Was it easier to lead or follow? Explain.

How did the exercises in previous chapters prepare you for this activation?

How did this exercise make you grow?

MINISTRY LEADER

What did you observe from your ministry members?

____

____

____

____

____

____

____

____

____

What type of constructive criticism did you provide?

____

____

____

____

____

____

____

Did any of your members find it extremely difficult to complete this exercise? If so, how did you handle that?

____

____

____

____

____

____

____

____

____

What did you notice during the transitions?

____

____

____

____

____

____

Did you observe how the members followed in comparison to them leading?

How were the signaling, transitions and patterns?

ADDITIONAL NOTES

Chapter 5
I've Got a Question

Well, we have endeavored through some serious research and are now at the part of the book/workbook that addresses questions. I will not answer each question in the book as this workbook is meant to provide a tool for deeper study. Many of the questions posed in the book were philosophical in nature and did not lend themselves well to a workbook.

Here is a list of questions that should help you prepare yourself as well as the ministry.

INTRODUCING A DANCE MINISTRY

Why do you want to add dance to the worship service?

____

____

____

____

____

____

What scripture/scriptures speak of dance in the church?

____

____

____

____

What is the vision and mission of your church?

____

____

____

____

____

____

What is the foundational scripture for your dance ministry?

____

____

____

____

How does this scripture align with the mission and vision of the church?

How does your ministry support or advance the mission and vision of the church?

What type of ministry (evangelistic, apostolic) is your church? How does adding dance to worship support the ministry?

How was dance used in both the Old and New Testament?

What is your strategy for adding dance to the worship service?

Will you utilize the entire ministry or a select number of dancers during the worship service?

What is your rotation plan for the dancers?

____

____

____

____

____

____

____

What garments will be utilized during worship service?

____

____

____

____

____

____

What, if any, worship instruments do you currently have?

____

____

____

____

What worship instruments will you utilize?

____

____

____

____

____

____

What basic information will the ministry need to know if asked?

____

____

____

____

When would you like to implement this change?

____

____

____

____

____

____

At this point, you should have a good idea as to what the vision and mission are for the dance ministry. Go over some of the responses above and flesh out what these things mean to your ministry. Use your church's vison and mission statements as a guide. If you are unable to find one for your church remember this: the vision is where you see the ministry going, the mission is how you are going to accomplish the vision.

VISION STATEMENT

____

____

____

____

____

____

MISSION STATEMENT

____

____

____

____

____

____

Before setting up your meeting, please make sure that all aspects of your request align with the overall mission and vision of the house you are submitted to. God is not an author of confusion or division. If you find that your desires and the vision of the house are in conflict, you may need to rethink your approach. Each ministry should support and push the overall vision of the church body forward. I recommend you take some time to reflect and jot down your thoughts as to how you can realign your initial thoughts in such a way that they support the church you are currently submitted to.

REFLECTION

COMBINED REHEARSAL

I know many of your ministries have rehearsal on different days and different times. At some point, the dance ministry needs to join the worship team rehearsal to learn how to flow together. The following questions are to help you assess your rehearsal time with the worship arts ministry. I encourage you to have your minister of music as well as the psalmist answer the questions provided. This will provide great insight for the ministry as a whole.

How did the psalmists/singers respond to your presence?

____

____

____

____

How did the dancers flow with the worship team?

____

____

____

____

____

____

What was your comfort level trying to dance while they rehearsed?

____

____

____

____

____

Were there songs being used that were unfamiliar? If so, did leaping from scripture or free worship prepare you to flow?

____

____

____

____

____

Where you able to understand the music? (Notes, structure, etc.)

____

____

____

____

____

____

Were you able to determine different components to the song (vamp, chorus, bridge)?

____

____

____

____

____

____

MINISTER OF MUSIC

What were your thoughts about the dancers joining rehearsal?

____

____

____

____

____

____

____

Were you distracted by them? Explain.

____

____

____

____

____

____

____

Were you able to see the full picture of worship by adding them to your rehearsal time?

____

____

Have you ever attended one of their rehearsals?

____

____

____

What are your thoughts about allowing the dance ministry leader to provide a teaching on the ministry of dance to the entire worship arts ministry?

____

____

____

____

What are some of the barriers that are present within the worship arts ministry?

____

____

____

____

____

____

____

____

____

____

What initiatives have been or will be put in place to bridge those gaps?

____

____

____

____

____

____

____

PSALMISTS

Was having the dancers present a distraction for you? Explain.

____

____

____

____

____

What are your thoughts about having the dancers join rehearsal on a consistent basis?

____

____

____

____

____

____

Have you ever heard a detailed teaching on the ministry of dance? If so, what do you recall?

____

____

____

What are some of your thoughts (good or bad) concerning the ministry of dance?

____

____

____

____

____

____

____

____

Explain the function of the dance ministry to the worship arts ministry?

____

____

____

____

____

____

What has been some of your experiences with the dance ministry?

____

____

____

____

____

____

____

____

____

____

The above questions should have given you some much-needed insight into your worship arts ministry. Now that you have several answers, it is time to work out a strategy. Perhaps you found out that the there is a gap in knowledge as it relates to the ministry of dance. Maybe the psalmists are distracted by the glory they see when you minister. Better yet, the minister of music was not aware that there was a disconnect in the ministry. You are now in the perfect position to fill in those gaps. The first step is knowing; now you must act upon it.

What did you learn from the answers above?

____

____

____

____

____

____

What areas require deeper study as a ministry?

____

____

____

____

____

____

____

How can you assist the Minister of Movement?

____

____

____

____

What areas/aspects of the worship arts ministry worked well together and which areas of the ministry need improvement?

____

____

____

____

____

____

____

____

____

MINISTRY LEADERSHIP

Does the Praise and Worship dance leader have to minister in dance or be able to minister in dance?

Hopefully, you found the response in ***WPMW*** beneficial. I want to delve into the attributes that make a leader effective. Ideally, each ministry in the church is led by someone not only interested in the area they are charged to lead but who also have some experience or a skill set that supports their leadership role.

What leadership skills should be evident in all ministry leaders?

____

____

____

____

____

____

If not a dancer, what are some areas of study that would be beneficial?

____

____

____

____

____

____

____

Typically, the dance ministry leader has many areas of responsibility. Some of these include, but are not limited to, choreographer, Bible study leader, prayer leader, creating schedules, garment selection, song selection, accountability, conflict resolution, and they are ultimately responsible for the overall growth and development of the ministry (spiritually, physically, and technically).

What roles on the ministry could be delegated?

What are some negative implications that could present themselves if the leader is not a dancer?

How could the ministry leader incorporate outside help to grow the ministry and themselves?

What regional or national conferences could the ministry attend as a whole for growth and development?

ADDITIONAL NOTES

Closing Thoughts

I want to thank you for taking this journey with me. I count it an honor that you invested not only in my dream but in your own ministry. This has been such an eye-opening experience for me as a writer and as a minister of movement. When I started writing, I never imagined the demand would push me into a workbook. This whole adventure has been overwhelming. Yes, I said adventure, as it surely feels like one.

I want to encourage you to leap. Step out of the boat and into the waves to do the thing that you know you have always desired to do, especially if it makes you nervous. Fear is a great motivator! It reminds you that you are still human, but what is amazing is when you overcome that fear. Allow the uncertainty to fuel you to move beyond your present place and into the unknown future, even if it is not successful. It is ok to fail as long as you fail forward.

I therefore, a prisoner for the Lord, urge you to walk in a manner worthy of the calling to which you have been called, with all humility and gentleness, with patience, bearing with one another in love, eager to maintain the unity of the Spirit in the bond of peace.

Ephesians 4:1-3

This project could not have been done without the support of the women in this picture. Cheron, Keira, Sara, Kimbalee, Triston, and Tonya. I am honored that you would lend your likeness to this project. This does not represent all who have pushed, prayed, fasted, and supported me during this process. I have an entire "tribe" of men and women that have been there from before the beginning. I will not attempt to name them all, but each of you are near to my heart. I do, however, want to extend a special thank you to those in this photo. Ladies, each of you rock, and I look forward to seeing each of you grow.

Made in the USA
Columbia, SC
01 February 2019